MILLION DOLLAR FOLLOW UP

A POWERFUL 7 TOUCH SYSTEM TO GET PEOPLE OFF THE FENCE

COACH MICHEAL BURT

CONTENTS

MILLION DOLLAR FOLLOW UP

A POWERFUL 7 TOUCH SYSTEM TO GET PEOPLE OFF THE FENCE

INTRODUCTION

For over 15 years now I've been called on to help sales teams and individuals around the world to get an elevation in their sales careers. I still remember like it was yesterday when I started my business at 31 years old with no loans, no lines of credit, and less than $7,500 in the bank. All I had was my confidence that I could use my talents to solve a problem in the world and people would compensate me for those talents and solutions. I knew I could create value that people would exchange money for. What I didn't have might surprise you.

I didn't have a plan of attack. I didn't have a selling system.

I didn't have an "explanation of services." I just had my confidence.

I quickly learned that I needed all of the above. I also quickly learned that I could get almost anyone excited when I was in front of them with my energy but after I left and all that "business chemistry" went away so too did the initial spark we felt for each other. I never sat back and thought about what the best way to revive that spark was until I begin to coach thousands of sales professionals only to learn they had the same problem I had. They didn't know how to "re- connect" the energy of that first initial attraction to push a person to a buying decision. They created an initial attraction and then let it fizzle out never to recapture it again.

I saw a stat once that I latched on to. It takes 7-15 touches almost 80% of the time to convert a prospect to a client. I begin to "touch" my prospects 7-15 times in a doggedly and persistent manner but many of them never pulled the trigger to a buying decision.

It wasn't my effort that was the problem. It was my methodology. I didn't know how to touch them in a meaningful way to create a buying decision or as Dale Carnegie once said "To arouse a genuine want or desire for my product or service."

Today I would tell you unequivocally that "money only changes hands when problems are solved." The follow up is an attempt to persuade the prospect that they have a real problem they need to take action on and that you are the perfect person in the world to solve that problem for them. The 7-15 touches continues to clearly articulate their want or desire to solve the problem and your want and desire to be the one who facilitates their bigger future. You are a "missing ingredient" to their future and you're a "must have" vs a "nice to have."

In this book I'm going to articulate my strategies for following up with the "farm club," these are people who have indicated interest in your services but you have yet to close. These people are "on the car lot" and have "raised their hands" and are going to buy from someone. Why not YOU? The follow up is an art. World class sales professionals perfect this art and reap the benefits of perfecting it. For those of you who break the sales cycle down and become world class at it you will separate yourself from being an amateur and become a professional.

I can't wait to get started with you because if you do just a small % of what I'm going to teach in this program you will make a lot more money and help a lot more people.

1

4 MISSING STRUCTURES OF SALES PEOPLE

I have spoken to, worked with, or coached thousands of those in the profession of sales. Just like a doctor who sees patients daily you begin to see patterns. Although you may think your business is unique (something everyone tells me on the front end) it's not. The purpose of ANY business is to create a customer. Every day you either take action toward creating a customer and toward your sales goals or you take actions that are not toward creating a customer and your sales goals. We separate this out into two categories:

1. **High Value Activity** - Specific and intentional activity that is in alignment with the highest use of your time toward creating customers and generating new revenue.

2. **Low Value Activity** - Specific activity that is NOT in alignment with the highest use of your time toward your sales goal and DOES NOT generate new revenue.

Lots of sales people spend lots of time in ACTIVITY but it's LOW VALUE ACTIVITY.

My goal is to get you doing a minimum of three High Value Activities per day on any day that is a money generating day. I learned this many years ago from famed business coach Mark Leblanc.

As I see it there are FOUR BIG MISSING STRUCTURES for most sales professionals around the world:

1. They do not have a world class "Explanation of Services" therefore they don't have anything valuable or differentiated to say. This places them into a commodity trap.

2. They do not have a coordinated and systematic attack on new customer acquisition. This leaves them floundering daily on "how to get a new customer" and relying on too few strategies to get their phone to ring.

3. They do not have a disciplined or consistent follow up mechanism in place to get prospects to a buying decision. This leaves lots of money on the table that could be in their pocket if they knew how to follow up appropriately.

4. They do not create a customer experience that drives deep advocacy after the experience and referrals. 98% of people never follow up with a customer once they have done business with them. This causes the customer to forget about the experience and there is nothing to "re-kindle" the initial attraction.

All of my coaching goes to work on these four big missing structures

2

BIG 4 OF MY LEGACY SELLING SYSTEM

Every sales professional needs a "selling system." This could be called a "customer generation system" to drive new leads and acquire customers. Early in my career I didn't have one of these so we had big months and bad months. It was because we didn't have a consistent and systematic approach to creating new leads and generating energy.

Always remember that money follows four things:

1. Attention - If you can't get any you can't sell anything.

2. Energy - What kind are you creating? Low or high?

3. Circulation - Constant and consistent movement and perpetual movement. It does not follow stagnation.

4. Activity - Coordinated and calculated activity toward the dominant focus.

Money ONLY changes hands when problems are solved. The bigger the problem the more people will pay to solve it. You can solve small problems for small people but expect to get paid in small ways. You can solve the same problem for bigger people and they will compensate you in much bigger ways. The first big homebuilder I worked for had a big problem:

He went from selling 40 homes per week to less than 4 per week.

He was willing to pay me $120,000 to solve his problem.

Some people have problems but won't spend one dime on solving them. You have to ask yourself these questions:

1. What problems do we solve?

2. For whom do we solve them for?

3. Who would compensate us the most?

4. Who do we love solving problems for?

I believe in moving from a defensive posture to an offensive mobility. This means each week we need to be in a forward acting position vs. waiting on something to happen. Nothing has to happen to us for us to take action and create something positive.

Because of this belief I have developed a selling system, a calculated and coordinated way to generate customers. It has four main parts to it:

1. We start every week of with a HIT LIST- These are targets of people we believe we can "help" with our services. My goal is 10 new ones per week.

2. We have a FARM CLUB- These are people who have indicated interest in our services that we have not closed. This is where the MILLION DOLLAR FOLLOW UP comes in with seven great touches.

3. We have a TOP 25- These are BIG ADVOCATES who know us, love us, and actively advocate for us. Our goal is to build 25 of these who will send us on average of 3-6 referrals per year.

4. We have a NET PROMOTER STRATEGEY- This is a strategy to take our current customers to people who promote us with positive energy due to the customer delivery we offer of solving their problems in unique ways.

Our offensive strategy then is this:

1. Target 10 people for the HIT LIST weekly we want to get the attention of and share our Explanation of Services with to see if they are interested.

2. Target 5 people we are trying to CLOSE each week in our FARM CLUB with our MILLION DOLLAR FOLLOW UP strategy.

3. Touch 3 of our TOP 25 per week with a meaningful value exchange to stay top of mind.

4. Onboard all new CUSTOMERS through our NET PROMOTER strategy properly and continually add value so they are referring us. (Typically we have 2-5 of these per week).

This creates at least 20 HIGH VALUE ACTIVITIES that puts us playing offense vs. defense weekly. This is part of our Selling System. I unpack the entire system in my book "Everybody needs a Coach in Life" and in my "Total Growth Academy."

3
EXPLANATION OF SERVICES

How you explain your services matters. You will get hundreds, if not thousands of opportunities throughout your work life to explain "what you do." It will be one of the main questions you get asked any time you meet a new person. It will be the DEFINING moment when making a sales pitch if the prospect says yes to you or not. Most people never take ONE MINUTE to work on their explanation of services.

We believe that people do business with other people that believe the same things we do.

We believe that having something to say is just as important as having somebody to say it to.

We believe that with a world class EOS we can know in the first 15 seconds if we have a real prospect (someone that believes the same things we do) vs. having to chase someone for 15 months.

We believe a strong EOS has six parts to it:

1. Tell me what it is you BELIEVE....

2. Tell me WHY you BELIEVE it......

3. Tell me WHAT you really do as a results of your BELIEFS (How can you help me)

4. Tell me HOW you do it DIFFERENTLY than everybody else we may look at.

5. Tell me WHO you have done it FOR so I know you are legit.

6. Ask me this question: If I could do it for you just like I've done it for all these other people what would stop us from doing business with each other?

The EOS gets you out of the commodity trap. It separates you by helping you to articulate who you are, what you believe, why you believe it, what it is you really do, how you do it differently than everybody else, and there is an ASK at the end.

Without a proper or well thought EOS how do you market yourself, position yourself, or differentiate yourself.

Remember, people do business with other people who believe the same things they do.

Go to work on this ONE tool and you will walk away with clarity, confidence, and total authority as an expert in your field.

4
PURPOSE OF THE FOLLOW UP

If money only changes hands when problems are solved what is the real purpose of the follow up? From my opinion the follow up serves these purposes:

1. It helps to articulate how YOU can solve the problem better than anyone else

2. It "re-kindles" the initial attraction and business chemistry between you and the prospect

3. It makes the prospect STOP and THINK of how you can be a unique asset to them

4. It challenges them to look at their problem with a new perspective

5. It "triggers" a buying decision from the prospect

Now, this is how most people follow up:

1. I was just thinking about you

2. I just wanted to "check in"

3. I woke up with you on my mind (This one is CREEPY)

4. I was just doing my due diligence

5. I wanted to see if you had any more questions

6. I'm ready to go, are you ready to go?

Now, does any of these move you to a buying decision? How many of you are guilty of following up like this? They do NOTHING to help people understand how you are uniquely qualified to help them.

The purpose of the follow up is to move someone to a buying decision. An object at rest will stay at rest unless acted on by an outside force (you). It takes 7-15 touches 80% of the time to convert a prospect to a buyer.

We talk a lot about "The current of the urgent" in our book "Zebras and Cheetahs." This current is phone calls, text messages, Facebook messages, LinkedIn pings, Snapchats, and more. We are in a fight for one thing with our prospects: ATTENTION.

Calling with no value is seen as a nuisance in today's world. Call with a thought. Call with an action. Call with a challenge. Call with an idea. Call with a strategy. Call with a referral.

But never, and I mean NEVER call with nothing to say but, "I just wanted to check in."

5

5 TYPES OF SALES PROFESSIONALS

In the book "The Challenger Sale" the social scientists determined after studying over 6,000 sales professionals that there were five types and one type represents up to 40% of the top players. I want to tie these types in to a style of follow up I call "The Challenger."

1. **The Relationship Builder** - Always wants to be liked by the customer or prospect and gives up most if not all of the control. They would be the one with the terrible follow up.

2. **The Hard Worker** - Comes in early. Stays late. Makes the required 100 phone calls but has nothing valuable to say and can't move a prospect off the fence.

3. **The Reactive Problem Solver** - Is good at solving problems for customer AFTER they are a customer but not good at actually getting a customer.

4. **The Lone Wolf** - Keeps to his or her self. Plays by their own rules. Disliked by most in the group and a managers nightmare. They do get results but builds serious enemies along the way.

5. **The Challenger** - Considered a true expert. Takes control of the ENTIRE process. Challenges the prospect to think and take action. Begins coaching the minute they have an opportunity. Challenges the status quo and brings unique and differentiated perspectives that lead to real results.

When I ask people all over the world which one they believe WINS the most guess what they tell me? The Relationship Builder. We are taught from an early age to fit in vs. stand out, to be liked vs. respected, and to go with the flow. We are not taught to "rock the boat," "challenge the status quo," or to "make people think."

This is precisely why I think most drop the ball on the follow up.

I do want to be liked but I'd rather be respected for my expertise, acumen, and the results the prospects can sense I can get for them. This is why I love the Challenger model. The stats tell us that 40% of ALL TOP PERFORMERS are

Challengers. Only 6-10% of the top performers represent most of the other four.

When I follow up with a prospect who has indicated interest in my services I do one thing: Challenge them.

Challenge them to do what you ask?

1. Think of a better way

2. Be open to my possibilities

3. See how I can help them

4. Show them how our process is better than someone else

5. To see how they could be producing at much higher levels

6. To create a sense of urgency to make a buying decision

7. To see how my past experiences make me uniquely qualified to solve their problem

8. To build an affinity with me, my message, and my methodology

9. To see me as an asset vs. a liability (One adds and one subtracts)

To challenge another person you may or may not know that well you have to show a "demonstrated capacity" to help them. This is why having a strong ability to articulate, listen, synthesize, pivot, and respond quickly is vital to your long term success and your follow through.

Instead of wanting to be liked instead seek to solve the problem with the follow up. Show them problems or "missing structures" they don't even know they have. Offer them a solution that SIGNIFICANTLY alters their future.

You won't be able to do this if you don't know what you are talking about, don't have valuable information to offer, or can't pivot when they push back.

6

CURRENT OF THE URGENT

I mentioned the "Current of the Urgent" earlier in the book but you've got to known what you are really fighting for which is attention. Because of an overload of information I can meet you, be incredibly interested in your products or services, be close to a buying decision and then completely push you to the bottom of the pile of decisions in less than one day. What you are really fighting for is their undivided attention on you, your product, and your service and you have to be a PRIORITY.

Jill Konrath in her book "SNAP SELLING" book did a fantastic job articulating it this way.

A prospect is constantly vacillating back and forth on this:

1. Your service is SIMPLE or NOT.

2. Your service is INVALUABLE or NOT.

3. Your service is ALIGNED with what we are doing or NOT.

4. Your services is a PRIORITY or NOT.

You can be IN today and OUT tomorrow.

I once pitched my services to a person who bought EMOTIONALLY for $75K on a Friday afternoon. I left excited for a new contract and new revenue only to get a cold shower by Monday morning when he informed me that over the weekend he had been SUED by one of his employees and faced a huge TAX LIABILITY. Our deal was over.

Your real goal here is to GET and KEEP your prospects attention while they are HOT and not let it go. Once you've lost it you are in a downward spiral fighting for relevance you may never get back. We must stay at the top of their mind constantly with cues, nudges, bumps, and invites. Never let DEAL FATIGUE set In due to your negligence of not following up and staying relevant.

7

7 TOUCH FOLLOW UP SYSTEM

When I was a championship basketball coach I could tell you that 90% of the time we won based on just three stats:

1. We had less than 14 TO's in a game.

2. We gave up less than 7 second shots in a game.

3. We stopped our opponent 21X in a game in increments of three stops (This killed momentum).

Because of these stats we practiced to these weekly and tracked everything.

Selling is a game of probability. You are trying to increase the probability of making a sale by:

1. Crafting a world class EOS.

2. Working a true selling system.

3. Cultivating the discipline of a seven touch follow up.

4. Creating an experience that drives refer-ability.

The stats tell us that it takes 7-15 touches to a prospect to convert them to a client 80% of the time. If this is true why wouldn't we all have a great seven touch system?

Now that we know HOW to follow up (The Challenger) we must put a great touch system in place that moves a person to a buying decision.

TOUCH #1 - Get their attention. I use referrals to do this. I use video to do this. I cold call with high energy. I use connectors to open the door. I use past clients. I use strong e-mails. I will use anything I need to in order to get someone's attention.

TOUCH #2 - Get a commitment for a face to face. Face to face is where the magic happens. If you can't get a face to face or SKYPE get a dedicated time to talk and visit about how you can solve their problem. This is where I share my EOS.

TOUCH #3 - Send a SUMMARY of the meeting and commitments and action steps. You said you would do this, I said I would do this, here are my recommendations. Put a target date and timeline.

TOUCH #4 - Phone Call to re- commit to the first meeting or follow up points. Have you had a chance to do this or that? We lose 10% of momentum every day we don't take action. Create a sense of urgency.

TOUCH #5 - Show proof of concept. Use another related scenario of where you were successful doing for them what you are proposing here. We use testimonial videos here as well.

TOUCH #6 - Have your best client call them. Get one of your TOP 25 to pick up the phone and convince the prospect to take action and create a sense of urgency by offering a credibility indicator.

TOUCH #7 - Take it Away. Here is how I speak to a prospect on touch #7:

Have you noticed how hard we have worked to earn your business?

Has anybody else worked this hard? (The answer is always NO)

You and I believe the same things. I've showed you what it is we can do for you. I've also showed you how we do it differently and the kinds of people we have done it for.

What is stopping you from taking action?

Or you can say, "If you're not ready to take action can you tell me why?"

Here's my philosophy: I'm only looking for people who are looking for me. I'm not going to chase or try and convince someone who doesn't believe the same things I do to do business with me. There are over 7 Billion people on Planet Earth. Some will buy, some won't buy, so what?

After seven touches you should know if you have a real prospect or not. At this point you can make a decision if you want to continue to touch 15 or not but it's a continuation of this process of challenging, drawing attention to the solution, and staying at the top of their mind.

I know what you're thinking. How long is this process? Well, it depends. It can be one week or one year. It all depends on the VELOCITY of the deal. This is the INTENSITY of the situation.

I've worked my seven touches in two weeks and I've gone two years with some people if I believe we could create magic together.

8
OBJECTIONS & REBUTTALS

I see lots of wimpy objections. They are really not objections but soft complaints. A professional who BELIEVES in himself and his product should be able to hold his own when there is push back.

When a person objects to pricing I agree. Yes, this is a good size commitment but it's nothing compared to the outcome. A bank invested $150K in me in 2009 and their return in a one-year cycle was $2.1 million. Would you make that investment?

I never lower my price. I always increase the value. These are common statements you would hear me say:

- "We lose 10% of momentum every day we don't take action."

- "We can have this conversation now or we can have it six months from now."

- "If you're not the decision maker who is and let's talk to them."

- "There is a power in taking action."

- "If you have to sleep on it you probably won't be able to sleep in it (real estate)."

- "What more is there to think on?"

- "You already bought, not let's make it official."

- "I can't help you until you commit."

If you think these are too strong here's what I would ask you? Do you believe in you and your product or service or not? If you do believe in you then why would you have a hard time helping a person come to a buying decision?

The Challenger pushes back when people offer lame excuses, small objections, or bogus comments.

9
HOW TO PUSH YOUR PROSPECT TO MOVE

I grew up in the south where we were taught to think things but not say them. We were taught to be "relationship builders" who don't rock the boat or create tension. We hate potential conflict. I go to NJ once per month to coach the largest bank in Jersey and they always say what's on their mind. There is no filter.

A relationship builder wants to be liked.

A challenger creates a "healthy tension" between himself and the prospect.

This helps you from getting stuck in the "friend zone." You know what I'm talking about right? This is where the prospect likes you, takes lunches with you, hangs out with you, and may even refer you but never actually uses your services. It's because somewhere along the way you have placed yourself in an inferior position. My best friends in the world pay for my coaching services. I use my best friends and pay their full commission structures because they are the best. If people are not using you it's because you've positioned yourself poorly and as a friend, but not an expert.

One of my top investment advisors in NJ says this within the first minute of sitting down with a prospect:

I believe that by the end of this meeting you and I will be doing business with each other. Let me dig in to your account and find where I can make you more money.

BAM. That's it. He doesn't just think it he says it.

No sales flirting. No beating around the bush. No sugar coating.

He just challenges the prospect and puts himself in a superior position as an expert from the beginning.

Just remember, soft touches do not move a person off the fence. It's okay to create a "healthy tension" to get some movement. So, how do you do that?

You challenge the prospect by doing two things:

1. Use statements that make them stop and think.

2. Challenge their current way of thinking to open them up to your possibility.

Sometimes I say things like:

- "I brought you exactly what you wanted."

- "If you're not ready to do business or take action can you tell me why?"

- "We can have this conversation now or six months from now."

- "You are losing the forward momentum of this deal."

- "I can't help you until you sign on the dotted line and then I won't let you fail."

- "Look at the results I'm getting for all these other people."

The point here is simple. If you don't challenge the prospect they won't give you the time of day and they will continue to treat you like the amateur you are acting like.

Here's another example. I fly a lot around the country to coach and speak. I hate flying commercial due to airport lines, customers who try and pack an oversized bag into the compartments one the planes, delayed flights and time away from my family. Because of this problem (remember that money only changes hands when problems are solved) I went exploring private aviation.

Many of the private charter companies charge an initiation fee to even have the privilege of flying on their plans and these fees could be $15-$30K. In anybody's world this is a lot of money. So I go on to their sites, show interest, ask to speak to a sales rep and have a conversation with each of them exploring. You should see how pitiful the follow ups have been that have done NOTHING to move me off the fence, think, or make a buying decision. Here is a typical follow up:

Hi Coach Burt—

I'm sorry I missed you today (he apparently called my phone) and I just wanted to follow up to see if you had any questions about our aviation options and private travel for you? If you do please give me a call.

This did absolutely nothing for me except provide an example of how NOT to follow up. What he should be saying is something that touches me "emotionally" and makes me think like this:

- "Coach Burt, we routinely get fathers back 25-40 days per year to spend with their four year old daughters."

- "Coach Burt, we helped another professional coach just like you save 2,000 hours this year in wasted time at airports. He converted that time in to $2 million dollars."

- "Coach Burt, did that two stop trek to New Jersey suck again? We could have you there in two hours vs. one full day."

You see how this makes me think? This is how he should be following up vs. these wimpy e-mail drips. It looks like I have a new prospect doesn't it?

10
SCRIPTING TO CLOSE A SALE

The professional sales professional wants one thing: CONTROL. Because he is such an expert he knows how to get it. For example here are some comebacks when dealing with the sales flirting and scripts I personally use to push people:

"I only have 20 minutes to spend with you to pitch your services."

ME: "Good, I've only got 18 and when

I'm done you'll be ready to go to round two."

"I need to talk to my wife and think about it."

ME: "In my house, my wife and I have such a strong relationship that she trusts my business decisions. She leads the house and I lead our business. I don't have to consult with her on every decision."

"I need to sleep on it."

ME: "If you have to sleep on it you probably ain't going to sleep in it. This is a fluid market and we are moving fast. Someone else will likely take this opportunity."

"Let me review the website."

ME: "Why would you want to review the website when you're talking to me live. I'm the one who created ALL the content on the website. Ask me any question you need to ask."

"This is just not in our budget."

ME: "Have you ever eaten at a great steak house and went over budget because the food was just that good? Of course you have. You can dine on filet mignon or .99 hamburgers but you always get what you pay for."

"This is not a good time for me to talk."

ME: "Well, it wasn't a good time for me to call either but you asked me to call you. Now you have my cell number. Call me the first minute you have free because I've got something important to talk with you about."

"This is not quite what I want."

ME: "I believe in the 80% principle. My wife and I moved in to a beautiful spec home that had 80% of what we wanted. I found out that 80% was worth every single dollar we spent on it."

"The timing is just not right."

ME: "I fought the same thing when I retired as a successful high school basketball coach but I finally decided that we create the timing. It will never be right to take action until you do it."

"This is just too expensive."

ME: "You are focused on the wrong number. This purchase will make you back 3X this amount and that should be the number you focus on. The way you are looking at this is all wrong. Something that makes you money is not an expense or liability, it's an asset."

"You don't work in my industry so you don't understand the uniqueness of it."

ME: "That's right. I don't drink the Kool- Aid of everyone in your industry. It usually takes the help of an outsider to offer real feedback because they are not biased or influenced by what they see every day like those in your industry do."

In every scenario I have a comeback to these low level objections. I hear them every single day. The key thing to focus on here is to challenge THEM to STOP and THINK. Many objections are just reflux time motions they are used to giving people who ACCEPT THEM.

You are not those people. You are a professional who is an EXPERT. They are coming to you for a reason. Maya

Angelo once said, "When we know better we do better." It's your job to help them "know better so they can do better." Steve Jobs always said that "The customer never knows what they want until you tell them."

We didn't know we wanted an iPhone or iPod until he showed us.

It's your job to show people that you can and will help them get to a better position in life due to your unique experiences, knowledge sets, and skill sets.

Do you believe in you and your product or service or not? If you believe in it you'll quit accepting these low level excuses.

11
HOW TO MAP OUT & ATTACK A WEEK

I want to end this little book by teaching you how to move from a defensive posture to an offensive mobility. It's been one of the cornerstones of my career. As a former coach I used to teach my players how to get the ball to the midline in less than 2.3 seconds. We were going to shove that thing down your throat for 32 straight minutes until you cried "Uncle."

We should be doing the same thing in the business world. We should be attacking vs. being attacked. We should be the puncher vs. the counter puncher. We should be on offense vs. defense.

The way to do that is by going to work weekly from an offensive positon. It looks like this:

- Nightly planning in your Monster Producer Planner on:

    o   Your Hit list of **SUSPECTS** you believe you can **HELP** with your services (minimum of 3-5 per day or 10 per week)

    o   Your Farm club of **PROSPECTS** that have indicated interest in your services you are **GOING TO CLOSE** this week with your Challenger follow up methods (Goal of 5 closes per week)

    o   Your TOP 25 list of biggest advocates of which there are three you are going to add deep value to this week with your insight and strategies.

    o   Your Connectors (at least 2) you are going to reach out to for strategic alliance.

o   Your **NEW CUSTOMERS** you are on-boarding correctly to quickly drive to **NET PROMOTER** status.

o   Your S**HOWCASE** events where you get in front of small to large audiences to connect, showcase your talents, and bring energy to the group for future potential.

o   Your **VALUE ADDS** for the week for your networks, partners, or clients

This puts you on **OFFENSE** vs. **DEFENSE.** The opposite is you just going to your office and WAITING on something to happen.

Know this, an object at rest will stay at rest unless acted on by an outside force. I hope this little book with BIG ideas has challenged you to be that FORCE.

I believe you were created in your mother's womb for greatness. That you were created to expand and multiply and to take dominion over your area. You were not made to be meek and lowly and wait on something to happen.

You need to get in the game and fight for you and your business. Get out there and get the exposure you need to be successful and fight for the follow up. Stay at the top of people's minds by coming back again and again and triggering in them an intuitive that you have something of value to offer and you will be there when they need you the most.

Secret agents never become big time sales professionals.

Go to work on this follow up system and watch money flow into your pocket.